TOP FUEL
DRAGSTERS

BY DENNY VON FINN

BELLWETHER MEDIA • MINNEAPOLIS, MN

Are you ready to take it to the extreme?
Torque books thrust you into the action-packed world
of sports, vehicles, and adventure. These books may
include dirt, smoke, fire, and dangerous stunts.
WARNING: read at your own risk.

This edition first published in 2010 by Bellwether Media, Inc.

No part of this publication may be reproduced in whole or in part without written permission of the publisher.
For information regarding permission, write to Bellwether Media, Inc., Attention: Permissions Department,
5357 Penn Avenue South, Minneapolis, MN, 55419.

Library of Congress Cataloging-in-Publication Data

Von Finn, Denny.
Top fuel dragsters / by Denny Von Finn.
    p. cm. – (Torque. The world's fastest)
Includes bibliographical references and index.
Summary: "Amazing photography accompanies engaging information about Top Fuel dragsters.
The combination of high-interest subject matter and light text is intended for students in grades 3 through 7"
–Provided by publisher.
ISBN 978-1-60014-288-8 (hardcover : alk. paper)
1. Dragsters–Juvenile literature. I. Title.
TL236.2.V662 2010
796.72--dc22
                            2009013253

Printed in the United States of America.

CONTENTS

What Is a Top Fuel Dragster?

Top Fuel dragsters are among the world's fastest machines. These race cars can go from 0 to 100 miles (161 kilometers) per hour in less than one second. Top Fuel dragsters reach more than 330 miles (531 kilometers) per hour in a race. A race is just 1,000 feet (305 meters) long!

5

The races Top Fuel dragsters compete in are called **drag races**. Drag racing is a very popular form of auto racing. Drivers and their cars race one-on-one in a straight line. The cars used in drag racing are called dragsters.

Fast Fact

A Top Fuel dragster consumes 1.5 gallons (5.7 liters) of fuel per second.

Top Fuel dragsters get their name from the fuel they burn. Dragster engines do not burn gasoline. They burn a mixture of **nitro** and **methanol**. This mixture may not contain any more than 90 percent nitro. These liquids create twice as much power as gasoline when mixed together.

Top Fuel Technology

A Top Fuel engine can push a dragster to incredible speeds. The engine has eight **cylinders**. A **blower** sits on top of the engine. It forces air into the cylinders. This helps the engine burn more fuel and create more power. It is estimated a Top Fuel engine creates as much as 8,000 **horsepower**!

Fast Fact

The inside of a dragster engine is so hot that parts of it melt during a 5-second race!

blower

A Top Fuel dragster has large rear tires called **slicks**. Slicks are 36 inches (91 centimeters) tall and 18 inches (46 centimeters) wide. Drivers spin the slicks before each race. This is called a **burnout** because it creates a lot of smoke. The burnout leaves a layer of sticky rubber on the track. This helps drivers gain **traction** when they race.

A Top Fuel dragster's frame is made of lightweight **chromoly** tubing. It takes 300 feet (91 meters) of tubing to build the frame. The entire dragster weighs only 2,250 pounds (1,020 kilograms).

A dragster could easily flip over without **wings**. Air passes over the wings and creates **downforce**. Downforce pushes the dragster to the track. This keeps the dragster stable. It also gives it better traction.

wing

The Future of Top Fuel Dragsters

Safety is the biggest concern for the future of Top Fuel dragsters. The extreme power of their engines makes them very dangerous to drive. In 2008, races were shortened from 1,320 feet (402 meters) to 1,000 feet (305 meters). Officials think shorter races will decrease the chances of future accidents.

Fast Fact

Top Fuel dragsters go so fast that they need chutes to help them stop after a race.

Don "Big Daddy" Garlits is the most important figure in the history of Top Fuel racing. He helped create the first fireproof suit for drivers. He was also the first driver to race a rear-engine car. This is much safer for the driver than a front-engine car. Today, all Top Fuel dragsters have rear engines.

Fast Fact

Don Garlits was the first drag racer to go 270 miles (435 kilometers) per hour in a dragster.

NATIONAL HOT ROD ASSOCIATION
NATIONAL CHAMPIONSHIP
DRAG RACES
AWARD FOR
TOP FUEL ELIMINATOR

BIG
DADDY

Garlits is pushing for more safety features on Top Fuel dragsters. A Top Fuel dragster has an **open cockpit**. Garlits hopes Top Fuel dragsters will one day have a **canopy** to further protect drivers. People like Garlits will help make sure the sport remains safe so people can continue to enjoy the quick acceleration and blazing speeds of Top Fuel dragsters!

GLOSSARY

blower—a device that forces air into engine cylinders

burnout—the act of spinning tires before a race; this increases traction by leaving a layer of hot, sticky rubber on the pavement.

canopy—a high-strength, see-through cover that encloses a dragster's cockpit and protects the driver

chromoly—a very strong, lightweight kind of steel tube used for building race cars

cylinder—a hollow chamber inside an engine in which fuel is burned to create power

downforce—a physical force that pushes a dragster toward the track

drag race—a race where two cars race each other in a straight line over a short distance

horsepower—a unit for measuring the power of an engine

methanol—a liquid mixed with nitro for use as fuel in Top Fuel dragsters

nitro—a liquid mixed with methanol for use as fuel in Top Fuel dragsters

open cockpit—the unenclosed area where the driver sits

slicks—large, wide rear tires

traction—how well a dragster's tires grip the road surface

wings—large, flat panels at the front and rear of a dragster that help create downforce

TO LEARN MORE

AT THE LIBRARY

Doeden, Matt. *Dragsters*. Mankato, Minn.: Capstone Press, 2003.

Von Finn, Denny. *Dragsters*. Minneapolis, Minn.: Bellwether Media, 2008.

Zuehlke, Jeffrey. *Drag Racers*. Minneapolis, Minn.: Lerner Publications, 2008.

ON THE WEB

Learning more about Top Fuel dragsters is as easy as 1, 2, 3.

1. Go to www.factsurfer.com.

2. Enter "Top Fuel dragsters" into the search box.

3. Click the "Surf" button and you will see a list of related Web sites.

With factsurfer.com, finding more information is just a click away.